Squirrels

Written by Gale Clifford 🐝 Illustration by Dominic Catalano

WEST
SIDE
PARK

There are squirrels in the city.

There are squirrels here and there.

3

There are squirrels in the flowers,

and squirrels everywhere.

I looked at a squirrel

and a bird in a tree.

But the squirrel and the bird

did not look at me.

I looked at a squirrel.

It was running on the ground.

It was hiding nuts for the winter.

How many has it found?

11

I looked at a squirrel

in the flowers near a tree.

And when I looked again,

it was looking back at me. 13

I looked for more squirrels.

I looked everywhere.

But the best squirrels I found

were in the clouds in the air.